My Childhood Under Fire

A Sarajevo Diary

My Childhood Under Fire

A Sarajevo Diary

Nadja Halilbegovich

Kids Can Press

Kids Can Press acknowledges the financial support of the Government of Ontario, through the Ontario Media Development Corporation's Ontario Book Initiative; the Ontario Arts Council; the Canada Council for the Arts; and the Government of Canada, through the BPIDP, for our publishing activity.

Published in Canada by
Kids Can Press Ltd.
29 Birch Avenue
Toronto, ON M4V 1E2

Published in the U.S. by
Kids Can Press Ltd.
2250 Military Road
Tonawanda, NY 14150

www.kidscanpress.com

Edited by Charis Wahl
Designed by Marie Bartholomew
Printed and bound in Canada
All interior photos courtesy of the Halilbegovich and Morrison families.

This book is smyth sewn casebound.

CM 06 0 9 8 7 6 5 4 3 2 1

3 1969 01754 6622

⌐

Library and Archives Canada Cataloguing in Publication

Halilbegovich, Nadja, 1979 –
My childhood under fire : a Sarajevo diary / Nadja Halilbegovich.

ISBN-13: 978-1-55337-797-9
ISBN-10: 1-55337-797-4

1. Halilbegovich, Nadja, 1979– — Diaries—Juvenile literature.
2. Yugoslav War, 1991–1995 — Bosnia and Hercegovina — Sarajevo—
Juvenile literature. 3. Yugoslav War, 1991–1995 — Personal narratives,
Bosnian — Juvenile literature. 4. Sarajevo (Bosnia and Hercegovina)—
History—Juvenile literature. I. Title.

DR1313.32.S27H35 2006   949.703   C2005-903894-2

Kids Can Press is a *l©rus*™ Entertainment company

To all innocent victims of war
— especially children

Introduction

I have lived three lives.

In my first life, I lived happily with my parents and brother — a conventional middle-class family. We owned a comfortable fourteenth-floor apartment in Sarajevo and a cottage in the countryside, where we spent our weekends. My mother, Jasmina, was a business manager at the National Bank. My father, Sandi, worked for a large book company. At the end of my first life, my brother, Sanel, was graduating from high school, and I was a cheerful sixth grader.

My country, Bosnia and Herzegovina, was a part of Yugoslavia, located between Italy and Greece. The capital,

Sarajevo, was a beautiful, modern European city, ringed by breathtaking mountains. In 1984 it hosted a very memorable and magnificent Winter Olympics.

Everything changed on April 6, 1992. I was twelve. That morning I got ready for school and walked into the living room. My parents seemed troubled and sad. When I asked what was the matter, I could barely hear my mother whisper, "Nadja, you're not going to school today."

"Is it a holiday?" I asked, excited.

Again she whispered. "Nadja, it's the farthest thing from a holiday."

It was the beginning of war and of my second life.

My family spent the day in front of the television, unable to believe what we were seeing — groups of armed men in stocking masks setting up barricades throughout the city, blocking the streets. The next day the thunder of explosions and the whistle of bullets frightened us and our neighbors into the basement. There were more than 270 tenants in our apartment building, and we were all crammed into three small underground rooms.

Day after day we breathed the damp, stale air, watching in terror as the explosions made the ceiling above us shake. We stretched the last of our bread, crackers, jam and water. We became still and listless, like the sandbags stacked against the walls to protect us from shattering glass.

Finally, after weeks in the dark and cold basement, we could no longer deny the truth — war was here to stay.

On May 31, 1992, I opened my notebook and began to write. Instantly this diary became a friend who listened to all that I desperately needed to share. It was my only place of peace amid the chaos.

I am an adult now, living my third life in North America, but my diary is still my most valuable possession. It tells a small part of the story of my city, which struggled to breathe despite the noose of tanks and weapons determined to strangle it.

I often ask myself why I stayed alive when thousands of children were brutally killed. There is no answer. I know that nothing can bring them back, but only forgetting would make them truly dead. They will live in my heart and in the following pages as long as I live and share their stories.

May 31, 1992

The war is furiously raging through Sarajevo and my
homeland. Its first victim was Suada Dilberovic, a medical
student from Dubrovnik. Her young life was cut off by a
sniper at the Vrbanja Bridge. A great crowd had gathered
in front of the presidential building to protest the invasion.
From the roof of the Holiday Inn, snipers shot at unarmed
citizens who had come to demonstrate their desire to live
in peace and unity.

   I watched these war images on television and kept all my
sadness inside. Now, after nearly two months, I can no
longer bear all my piled-up feelings. This is why I write to
you, dear diary.

   Even at this moment, the deafening explosions jolt me
back to this cruel reality. Seeing my city being destroyed, I
feel a sharp pain in my soul. I don't understand why this is
happening to us. I desperately want to wake up from this
nightmare, but instead every dawn moans with the sounds of
air-raid sirens, and I head to the filthy basement. To wait.

June 1, 1992

It is unusually quiet this morning. For a moment it feels like peacetime, although I am not sure I remember how it feels to live in peace. School has been canceled for ages and I haven't seen any of my friends. Spring flowers have bloomed and I haven't seen them. But now air-raid sirens shatter this brief silence. I pack my book bag with some crackers, playing cards and my favorite teddy bear and head to the basement.

LOOKING BACK

During the first days in the basement, what scared me even more than the explosions that shook our building was that, for the first time, I saw my parents feeling hopeless and discouraged. All my life I had looked to them for advice, comfort and security. Suddenly, in the dark and dirty basement, the war had transformed my parents. When they tried to smile and reassure me, I could see the fear they couldn't hide. War had turned us all into frightened children.

June 2, 1992

Today is just another sad and bloody day of this monstrous war. We are living in constant fear.

Sometimes I think about my peacetime diary. It was full of cheerful memories and happy stories about adventures and vacations. Now I write about war—for myself and for my friends who left Bosnia. Maybe I could have gone, too. Many of our family friends warned us about the coming war, but we couldn't believe it would happen in our country. So we stayed, each of us trying to survive in our own way.

June 22, 1992

This is a day of great fear, sadness and death. Three civilians were killed near the National Bank where my mom works. Never in my life have I been so frightened. Choking back tears, I prayed that she would be all right. I called the Bank but couldn't say my mother's name because I was afraid of hearing terrible news. Fortunately she was okay.

Today on the streets of my beloved Sarajevo, nineteen citizens were killed and seventy-seven wounded.

July 4, 1992

Today, in a backyard, children were picking cherries. They were still unripe, but it was the first fruit the children had seen in months. Suddenly, a shell hit. Seven innocent children were killed — and only because they wanted a few cherries.

LOOKING BACK

During the bombings, our lifeline was the radio, and batteries quickly became the hottest item on the market. The radio told us what was happening in other parts of Sarajevo and the rest of the country. Through the radio we also received warnings from the Safety Department about the location of bombings and sniper activity.

But there were no children's voices. So one afternoon I phoned the radio station and said, "Hello, my name is Nadja, and I would love to read some of my poetry on the radio." The announcer was a bit taken aback, but she offered to record me. She kept replaying my poetry throughout the day. I felt deeply connected with my fellow citizens. Finally I had found a way for my voice to be heard after months of silencing it deep inside.

July 15, 1992

Today on National Radio I read something I wrote. I called it "War Spring." Here is part of it:

> The spring arrived quietly on its silky toes. It was afraid to wake up the mothers, fathers, sisters and brothers who now slept in the basement. The birds were not singing. The bees were not buzzing. Instead I heard explosions and the whistle of sniper bullets. Nobody was enjoying this spring. Children could not see the sun's smiling face. Everything was somber, hazy and gray.
>
> I want this war to be over soon, and I wish this war spring would disappear along with it.

July 29, 1992

Today is my thirteenth birthday. I am happy about it, but I know that at this very moment someone is grieving over a lost friend or family member. Friends from the building came to celebrate my birthday. I didn't invite my friends from other parts of Sarajevo — it would be too dangerous for them to go out on the streets. Still, we spent a beautiful afternoon talking, laughing and playing games.

My only wish is to celebrate my next birthday with all my friends in a free Sarajevo.

August 13, 1992

As I'm sitting in this dark and moldy basement, listening to
the sounds of exploding bombshells, I wonder ...
   Are those people in the mountains happy when they
shoot and kill? Do they feel sad about the people they kill
and the city they destroy? Do they shed a tear when they
see an old lady mourning her dead grandson? Do they feel
sorry about children's sad eyes and pale faces?

August 30, 1992

Around noon, citizens of the suburb of Alipashino
Polje were waiting in a long line for bread. A shell was
launched into the crowd, killing eight people and
wounding more than fifty. Right at that time, my father
was volunteering for the Red Cross. He had gone to pick up
rations of rice and flour with a group of neighbors. They
walked by the very place just minutes before the deadly
explosion and missed death by only a few steps.
   What a relief it was to see he was okay!

September 4, 1992

If there were peace, my friends and I would be getting
ready for the beginning of the new school year. We would

be rested and tanned. Instead, here we are, playing in the
hallways and stairwells of our apartment building. Our
faces are pale, with pink-violet shadows under our eyes.
Our shoes are too small. Each day we meet in a different
hallway so that we don't always bother the same neighbors,
although they are quite tolerant.

Today we are meeting with Mrs. Jasmina,
who will give us a knitting and sewing lesson.

September 7, 1992

Today we gathered in the basement. We brought lots of
colorful thread, needles, scissors and scraps of linen to
make stuffed toys with Mrs. Jasmina. We were cold, but
we had a lot of fun.

September 12, 1992

It's Saturday. Now that we are prisoners in this city under
siege, I've developed a sudden love for meadows, fruit trees,
vegetables, strawberries, raspberries and everything we had
at our cottage! I didn't like going there before the war
because of all the chores we had to do. I think you really
appreciate something only when you lose it.

I hope when this war is over and we become free, my family will spend many weekends at my favorite place: our cottage!

September 16, 1992

Today my friends and I, the Tenants of the Basement,
as we call ourselves, organized an exhibition of drawings
and handicrafts. We were all excited, and we told everyone
about the exhibition. We made special handmade invitations
for the eldest tenants of our building. I entertained
everyone with my guitar. What a beautiful exhibition!

LOOKING BACK

Early in the war, we had to get used to living without
electricity. No power meant no elevator to our fourteenth-
floor apartment, no lights, no television, no stove and no
bakeries, so we had to find a way to make our own bread.

It took a couple of months for Dad to strike a deal at a
flea market for a tiny copper stove that we could use on our
balcony. He finally got it in exchange for rice, a few bars of
soap and a can of oil. Until then, a generous neighbor on
the ground floor allowed all the tenants to use her wood
stove. Since the weather was still relatively warm, she
moved it into a small common area outside. Of course
everyone provided their own wood.

The stove instantly became a gathering place. Neighbors brought cushions, stools and chairs, and talked as they waited for their bread or pie to bake. My mom would make the dough and leave it for me to bake during the day while she was at work.

One day, when a few elderly women around the stove saw my bread, so anemic and flat, they muttered that my mom probably didn't know how to make bread. This was not true — during peacetime holidays, my mom made delicious bread.

So I asked the neighbor who owned the stove why my bread was so flat. "The yeast is probably stale," she responded. "I'll give you some of mine." The next day I went over to her apartment with flour and oil, and we made the dough using her yeast. In less than twenty minutes, the dough was bulging over the rim of the pan! I was so excited that I nearly dropped the heavy pan on my way to the stove.

Finally the bread was baked, with a beautiful golden crust. The same women were sitting around the stove, so I pointed to the bread and looked right at them.

"My mom made it!" I proclaimed.

September 26, 1992

My friends and I are exchanging war-food recipes created by our mothers with a bare minimum of ingredients. This afternoon Mom made some curious-tasting cookies out of cocoa, a bit of sugar and some stale corn flour. I shared them with all the children in the building. The cookies weren't nearly as good as the ones my mom used to make in peacetime, but we were all delighted to have something sweet. I dream of the day when we will be able to go out and buy ice cream!

LOOKING BACK

My brother was almost always hungry during the first year of the war. This made me sad, so I tried to think of ways to make dessert for him. In our humanitarian-aid rations, we sometimes received small juice-powder containers. When mixed with water, they made orange or blueberry juice. I would mix some of this powder with only a few drops of water to make a thick icing. Then I would take some crackers or bread and layer them with the icing to make little cakes. Sanel loved them!

October 1, 1992

No one in the world seems willing to save the people of Bosnia from extermination. The sharp cold is threatening to finish off the starved citizens. There are fewer and fewer trees in my city. Even the rare species that we carefully tended for so many years are gone. There are more and more obituaries in the newspapers, more and more crippled and wounded. Our doctors are trying to operate in conditions of a hundred years ago.

October 2, 1992

In today's newspaper I read about physical violence against young girls. Some people abuse children in a very bad and monstrous way. Those girls will always remember. They will always be afraid.

Is there anything human inside these so-called people? How can they do this and then look into the eyes of their own children?

October 3, 1992

The aggressor is still trying to take the city. The citizens of
the suburb of Grbavica are being driven out with only the
clothes on their backs. Many are being taken to concentration
camps. I feel deep compassion for these unfortunate people,
but I can't fully comprehend their fate. This war has brought
me a lot of suffering, but their tragedy seems unimaginable.

October 4, 1992

There is a great shortage of medicine in Sarajevo because
we're surrounded by tanks and the city is cut off. Many
citizens call the radio station and ask for the medicine
they need. We heard someone needed a medicine that my
family had, so Dad went to the radio station and donated it.

October 10, 1992

Today the aggressors bombed the Ljubica Ivezic
Orphanage. They killed three children and seriously
wounded thirteen — children who have already experienced
great hardships, living their childhood without parental
love and care. No human reason
can grasp this brutal crime.
 Why is this happening? I have no answer.

October 17, 1992

They call Sarajevo "the world's largest death camp." Soon
winter will take its toll. My heart breaks when I see an old
lady snapping off the branches of a bush and piling them into
an old, torn sack. So many people are hungry! They rummage
through the dumpsters, but how can they expect to find food
in dumpsters when there is no food in people's cupboards?

October 30, 1992

On the sunny and strangely quiet morning of October 18, I
begged my mom to let me go outside. I desperately needed
some warm sun. I begged and cried until she gave in. "Just
for a moment, all right?" she said. Already out the door, I
barely heard her. I flew down all fourteen flights of stairs.

Outside I just stood still, mesmerized by the beauty of
the world. Suddenly there was an explosion. Smoke and
dust were everywhere. I frantically looked around. Finally,
through thick smoke, I saw a large piece of our building
dangling in front of me.

I ran toward the entrance, screaming and crying. I
touched my leg and I felt blood. I also felt a sharp,
stabbing pain in my legs, but I kept running until I found
a neighbor. I threw my arms around her neck and she
dragged me to her door. Soon, a dozen neighbors were

crowded around, trying to help.
I was half-conscious, but I could
hear them through the confusion. Some
were screaming, some were trying to talk to me. I
didn't dare look at my legs, even though the neighbors had
already wrapped them with towels to slow down the bleeding. I saw my blood on the walls and on the floor.

Suddenly I recognized my father's voice. He took me in
his arms. I could hear his quiet moaning as he picked me
up. Then a kindhearted stranger offered to drive me and
other victims to the hospital. My father's shirt was soaked
in my blood. He kept gently hugging me to his chest and
gathering in my legs, as if afraid I would spill away. Half-
dazed, I whispered, "Dad, please don't let me lose my legs."

At the hospital, a nurse put me on a stretcher and took me to
a large room filled with the dead and wounded. All the beds and
stretchers, as well as the floor, were covered with bodies. I was
told to wait because victims worse off than me were being
rushed in every minute from all parts of the city. The boy next
to me was having a piece of shrapnel taken out of his back
without anesthetic. He kept trying to muffle his moaning by
covering his mouth. He was incredibly brave, so I stopped crying.

Eventually the doctor and nurse rushed over to me. They
slit open my pants and examined my legs. I had lost a lot of

blood, but my bones were not damaged, so they didn't have to amputate my legs. I began to cry. The doctor assured me that I would be able to go home and would not have to stay in the overfilled hospital.

Dad and I waited in the hospital hallway, hoping to get a ride from someone. Minutes later, fresh blood appeared on my legs, and I had to be re-bandaged.

While I was lying on a stretcher, a girl came and spoke to me. Her parents and brother were in the hospital, wounded by a shell that had hit their apartment. She had been injured, too, but had already healed. This gave me hope.

After an hour or so, my father's friend, a journalist, happened to drive by the hospital. He offered us a ride. As he and Dad carried me into the car, crimson stains blossomed through the bandages. Again I was rushed to the doctor, who put another set of bandages over the two previous layers. I felt sorry about all the bandages he used on me, because I knew there was a great shortage.

When we made it to our building, Sanel ran over, took me in his arms and started crying like a child. Only then did I truly realize how much we love each other. He carried me up all fourteen flights of stairs.

Painful days and sleepless nights followed. As soon as I closed my eyes, I saw smoke and blood everywhere. My mother fed me spoonfuls of food, like she did when I was small. Neighbors and friends visited me every day. Each one brought a rare treat — an apple, a carrot, a piece of chocolate or some orange juice. These were such wonderful and delightful luxuries. The elderly neighbors would bring me a piece of pie or bread they had baked. Everyone's kindness and care brought me back to life.

After some time, I no longer had to go to the hospital to have my bandages changed. Two visiting nurses came to dress my wounds and help me through the pain. The director and members of Palcici — the choir I belong to — sang and danced for me. They rekindled the hope that I would be able to dance with them again. I never felt lonely because there was always someone at my side.

Slowly I've recovered, but I've also changed. I'm more frightened and worried — and a lot older.

LOOKING BACK

I was unable to walk at all for two weeks. Sanel, Mom and Dad had to carry me to the bathroom several times a day. While Mom was at work and Dad out in search of food and water, Sanel had to carry me by himself. I was ashamed and frustrated at having my nineteen-year-old brother carry me to the toilet.

One day he and I were alone, and I was determined to get to the toilet by myself. I rolled off the bed like a sack of potatoes, hitting my elbows and shoulders on the floor. My legs were lifeless, so I used my arms to drag myself along. It was tiring, but I kept slithering on the carpet like a wounded snake.

Finally I arrived at the bathroom door and lifted myself up by bracing my arms against the walls. When I got to the toilet, I sat on the lid and caught my breath. I pushed back the sweaty strands of my hair and called out, "Sanel, guess where I am?"

"In your bed, of course. Where else?" he said.

"No, Sanel. On the toilet!"

Seconds later, he appeared wearing a smile of amazement. "You did it, Nadja. You did it!"

I felt so encouraged that I tried crawling back to bed. Sanel had to carry me a little way, but the next day I crawled again. Finally I started walking slowly with the help of Sanel's ski poles. No matter how many times I fell, my only thought was, I will walk again!

November 1, 1992

Today UNICEF declared the beginning of the Children's Week of Peace, and Palcici gave a concert. I am still walking with the ski poles, so I couldn't dance, but I announced all the songs. During the last song, I got carried away and tried to dance, but I lost my balance. My choir director was right there and caught me before I fell. After the show we were given an amazing treat of hot chocolate and croissants!

LOOKING BACK

Since I was nine, I had been a member of Palcici, the internationally known children's choir that toured throughout Bosnia, France and Italy. However, with the start of the war, some of its members fled the country with their families, and many others were not allowed to risk their lives on the streets to come to rehearsals. Our membership of a hundred young singers shrank to twelve.

At first we met at one another's apartments. Our choir director would bring his guitar, and we learned songs of hope and peace. Despite the bombings, we took our songs to hospitals, underground schools, kindergartens and orphanages. I was always deeply touched to see that our music brought a spark of light to the overwhelming sadness in the eyes of wounded and orphaned children.

Later we met at the recording studio of the National TV and Radio station. We taped our songs and also made several videos that were frequently shown on TV.

Singing and performing with Palcici was something I needed to do, not only for those who found comfort in our music but also for myself. Many other singers must have felt the same because gradually Palcici regained its pre-war size.

When explosions and bullets threatened to be Sarajevo's only music, the children fought back with song.

November 3, 1992

Today the aggressor broke the peace agreement promised for the Children's Week of Peace. Do children mean nothing to them? If they don't love somebody else's children, can they really love their own?

All we can find to eat is rice, macaroni and beans, so we don't get the vitamins we need. My family was given vitamin supplements by the humanitarian organization La Benevolencia. We are so happy and grateful.

November 4, 1992

The only certain thing is that winter is coming. We are promised plastic sheeting for our broken windows. We hope it will keep us a bit warmer.

November 5, 1992

Our dear zoo is gone! Its last inhabitant, the brown bear, died of hunger today.

November 6, 1992

Most of the trees have been cut down for firewood, so we can't see the leaves changing to beautiful autumn colors. But we welcome the rain, as we can collect the water.

Death is the most frequent passerby on the streets. Life seems cheaper than a slice of bread or a cup of water. Despite all this, Sarajevo lives.

November 8, 1992

Schools, nurseries and museums— all things that symbolize culture, knowledge and education— are being destroyed. Our classes are held in improvised classrooms in basements and apartments.

Today some citizens were given an aid package of food by the humanitarian organization Merhamet. Because I was wounded, I received one, too. I am very grateful, but I know there are thousands more who need the same care.

LOOKING BACK

It was very cold sitting in the basement for four hours straight for our classes. It was hard to concentrate when we were always rubbing our hands, ears and noses to keep warm. Everyone brought something to burn in the stove — bits of furniture, even a handful of piano keys. I brought some of Mom's shoes. Someone brought a piece of car tire, but the burning rubber smelled terrible. Despite the cold, we enjoyed our classes — we could see our friends, and our lives seemed at least somewhat normal.

November 9, 1992

I am writing while looking at today's newspaper, *Oslobodjenje*. The eyes of a ten-year-old boy look at me innocently from a photograph. Adnan Sehic was outside with his mother, grandparents and uncle collecting wood. On their way home, a shell exploded. All Adnan saw

was smoke. All he heard were screams. He ran into a
nearby house. The others were all wounded, his mother
most severely. Nobody knows if she will survive.

Adnan is still in the hospital because of the injuries to
his legs. He is terribly worried about his mother, especially
because his father was run over by a train five years ago.
His seven-year-old sister is staying with their aunt. Adnan
received a doll from a lady who makes toys for little
patients. He plans to give it to his sister when she
comes to visit.

November 10, 1992

I can't shake off the image of Adnan's big dark eyes
from yesterday's paper. They are yearning and questioning,
Why all this? Why did the world let this happen to me?

They say that thirteen thousand children have been
killed in my country. Yet the world remains silent.

November 21, 1992

I am very cheerful today. We bought a stove and some
firewood. It will be warmer now.

November 30, 1992

Sarajevo sinks into the autumn rains. Sarajevo sinks into death and emerges again. Sarajevo fights and defends. Even though there is not a single family whose home sadness has not entered.

LOOKING BACK

Our apartment had comfortable, soft beds, but no one slept in them. Sleeping in a bed next to a window was very dangerous because the window could be shattered by explosions during the night.

The large wooden dining table was no longer used for family and friends; it was chopped into pieces to feed the stove. Even our once beautiful view of the mountains was now a threat — the mountains hid the tanks that were killing us.

December 2, 1992

No water, no electricity, no gas. There is nothing!

December 5, 1992

We are the future of this planet. We want to grow up
in freedom and happiness. Hey, you! Mankind! I am your
future, so STOP these bloody wars. Let your heart be filled
with warmth and love. Wouldn't it be wonderful if all the
children of the world walked to school singing? If only the
adults could become children. There would be no wars, no
suffering and slaughter. There would be no hatred or lies.

December 15, 1992

I have to tell you something very important. Today while
Mom and I were changing my bandages, we found a large
piece of shrapnel in a scab that fell off — the biggest
piece so far. I was lucky that the smooth side hit me, or
it would have damaged the bone.

    I decided to keep it as a souvenir. But when I think of
it — why do I need such a souvenir?

LOOKING BACK

It was the first New Year's Eve of the war. At midnight we
cheered and hugged, but as the bombs and gunshots began
to roar, we realized that instead of fireworks in the sky

there would be only smoke, fire and the sounds of war. Instantly our cheer turned to anxiety. My only New Year's resolution was to try to stay alive, and my only wish was that each person in the room lived to celebrate the next New Year.

January 1, 1993

I WISH YOU A HAPPY NEW YEAR! We spent New Year's Eve with our neighbors. We made soy sandwiches, mint cake, rice pastry, rice pie, rice wine and chocolate rice cake — there was rice in almost everything! We played music and danced. There were tears in our eyes when we wished each other a peaceful year. It is horrible to think like this, but not all of us may live to see peace.

May the old year be the last one of the war!

And may these pages reflect the happiness and peace in my soul.

January 15, 1993

Today, at 2:20 p.m., a deadly missile exploded in front of the Sarajevo Brewery, where citizens were collecting water. Eight killed and fifteen wounded! In a single second, two children were injured and lost both their parents.

If I had the right to live, which I do not, if I were somebody instead of a mere number, I would wish all aggressors, all enemies of children, to feel the same sadness and pain that they inflict on us.

An immeasurable sorrow overwhelms my heart. The citizens killed today died thirsty.

LOOKING BACK

Water was so precious. Each bucketful served many purposes. First, my mom used it to rinse the soap off the dishes. The water drained into a bucket to become soapy water for scrubbing the next day's dishes. After that, the water was used for cleaning the furniture and wiping the floors. Then my mom would clean the hallway on our floor. Finally we used the water to manually flush the toilet.

February 2, 1993

It is eight o'clock in the morning. We have electricity, so we're rushing about doing chores. Dad is bringing buckets of water up the elevator, Mom is baking bread, making supper and washing a load of laundry. Sanel is vacuuming, and I am helping Mom in the kitchen. My war school begins in half an hour. It is cold and we have to wear gloves. Still, I am very happy I will see my friends. I hope all of them will be there.

February 11, 1993

I am sorry that I have not written for a while, dear friend. I came up with the idea that I should write a letter to the president of the United States, Mr. Bill Clinton, on behalf of all children, asking for help. I read it today on the radio.

February 21, 1993

Today Palcici performed a concert at my school, but as soon as we started, shells exploded just a few yards away. We were frightened, but like real professionals we kept going, even though some of the audience left the concert before it was over. Everyone was frightened. After the concert, I quickly ran home.

March 5, 1993

Days, weeks and almost a whole year go by — it is as if we are never going to come out of this insane war. Sarajevo is more and more miserable. Food and wood supplies are meager, but I have become almost indifferent to my fate. All my tears have dried up. I have forgotten what morning was like when I wasn't wakened by the sound of shells. I have forgotten what a quiet day and a peaceful sleep are. I am getting used to this humiliating life, if you can even call it a life.

March 8, 1993

Today is International Women's Day. Mom is using the last supplies from the food package sent to us by the generous people from the French region of Alsace.

I received a beautiful present from my dad and brother: a red lipstick in a little case with a mirror. I made eleven cheerful cards for Mom's friends. Many of them cried when they received my cards, especially those whose children have left Sarajevo.

Since it's too dangerous to go to school, classes were broadcast over the radio. I was on the air, and I congratulated all the brave mothers of my country. My wish for them was that the next Women's Day be celebrated with their families in happiness and freedom.

Will my wish come true?

April 5, 1993

The days of the war pass, each like the last. There is
no electricity, no water, no firewood, no bread, no food,
no friends — not even our neighbor. Just yesterday he
wandered off in search of food, and he hasn't come back.

April 17, 1993

Today I was invited to attend the launch of the book
Mama, I Don't Want to Go to the Basement. It is a
collection of drawings, letters and poetry created by
the children of the war. Four of my poems are included.
I am very happy. This encourages me to continue writing.

LOOKING BACK

After some of Palcici's performances for dignitaries and
UN soldiers, there would be a reception. Servers would
walk around with huge platters loaded with incredible
delicacies — sandwiches, meats and cheeses. Every time
one passed, I would take one or two pieces, wrap some in
my napkin and sneak them home as a surprise for my
perpetually hungry brother.

May 12, 1993

Today is my dear brother Sanel's birthday. Mom and I made sandwiches and sweets. If only we had some Coke!

Sanel's friends arrived in the afternoon and they had a wonderful time. But we couldn't get him a present because there is no place to buy gifts.

May 30, 1993

Sarajevo is in chaos. The aggressors in the surrounding mountains are fiercely shelling the city. Today 20 citizens have been killed and 170 wounded.

May 31, 1993

It is mostly quiet today. When Mom came home from work, she said that the streets are covered with glass, piles of rocks and ripped steel. Even worse, there were scattered shoes, clothes and human remains.

June 2, 1993

As soon as I woke up, I started getting ready for the filming of *The Children's Television Show*, which featured Palcici today. We filmed from ten thirty to three thirty, and I was exhausted. When I came home, I couldn't eat because I had eaten a gigantic sandwich at the television station. At least it seemed gigantic. Before the war it would have been just a sandwich.

LOOKING BACK

During the second year of the war, teachers began broadcasting lessons over the radio. Friday was my favorite day of the week — radio quiz day. Children who had the luxury of radio batteries and a working telephone called in answers when the teacher posed a question. After several months of keeping score, the teacher would announce the ten best students. They would get gifts of books and candy.

Every Friday I would sit on the floor with the phone in my lap, nearly buried in books, dictionaries and encyclopedias. As soon as I heard the question, I would dial the radio station, but the line was often busy with so many children calling. So I tried to outsmart them by calling in before the teacher finished the question. Sometimes I got through but didn't know the answer. Other times Sanel and Dad would disagree with my response and would shout different answers into phones in different rooms! Poor teacher — there he was with three stubborn players on the line, each shouting into the phone! These moments were both comic and exhilarating. They let us escape our stark reality, even if only for a short time.

June 4, 1993

It's Friday. I am getting ready to call in for a quiz on the radio. I have not won any points so far, but I always have lots of fun on Fridays.

June 6, 1993

I've gathered the children from the building — we are going to make our own newspaper! We've decided to call it *Kids of Sarajevo*. Everybody has an assignment — some will draw pictures, some will write stories or poems. We will also include jokes, word puzzles and war recipes from our mothers. This is the way children fight for freedom — and we are having a lot of fun!

June 13, 1993

There is no bread in stores today because there is no electricity or water in the entire city.

I guess I've just gotten used to this crazy war because I decided to go to choir rehearsal. As I was getting ready, a shell hit very close to our building, and I realized that it was too dangerous to go out on the streets. Even now, bombs are falling nearby.

Oh, I almost forgot — I came in ninth place in the radio quiz. There is a party for the winners today, but I have no way of getting there and the shelling is still going on.

PASN STII?? (danger)

June 14, 1993

My mother went to work despite the shelling. I am so worried when she goes out. Sometimes I huddle by the front door until she comes back.

We've heard that our defenders are advancing in the battles across Bosnia, so the aggressors are taking their revenge on Sarajevo. They vent their anger on children and unarmed civilians.

June 15, 1993

I spent today playing guitar, reading a comic book and playing the game I received as a prize on the radio quiz. I even studied a little because there is not much to do. I can't go outside — to movies, to the store or anywhere else I used to. It's really boring.

June 17, 1993

I went to school, but it was canceled. Instead I listened to the radio school and drew. When you are bored, minutes go by so slowly that an hour seems like a year. This war seems to be lasting a century.

June 27, 1993

Today is my dad's fifty-first birthday. I made a card and some war-recipe cookies and put them in a cute box. I wanted to surprise him, so I set the box outside our apartment door, rang the doorbell and quickly hid inside. Dad asked me to open the door, but I said I was too busy. He thought this was pretty strange since I always rush to the door when anyone visits. He opened the door himself and was very touched to find his present. After he read my card, we shared the cookies.

June 28, 1993

Today is a lucky day. I learned to ride a bicycle! I also carried seven ten-litre containers of water up the 252 steps to the fourteenth floor! More than seventeen gallons in all.

LOOKING BACK

For months I didn't see a single piece of fruit. Then Sanel got a job as an interpreter for the United Nations, translating between Bosnian and English. When the soldiers asked him if he wanted to be paid in food or money, Sanel chose food. One afternoon, he brought me an orange. For hours I held it in my hand, laughing and crying. I felt as though I were holding the entire world in my hand.

July 5, 1993

A sniper is shooting nearby. Mom went to work in spite of the danger. Dad is out getting soil. Since there is no place to buy vegetables, we will try to grow a few on our balcony.

July 30, 1993

Yesterday was my fourteenth birthday, and I had a small party. We couldn't play, sing or talk loudly, as the neighbors a floor below us has just lost their son defending the Zuc Hill. We could hear them crying.

Still, sometimes my friends and I got carried away and talked too loudly, and Mom had to remind us to keep quiet.

August 12, 1993

Some people call the murderers in the hills "beasts" or
"animals." I think that even though animals are not human,
in many ways they are humane. Animals are often more
sensitive and loving than humans. They are devoted
friends. Those who kill children and the elderly, who bomb
hospitals and schools and orphanages are entirely inhumane.

August 31, 1993

I know I haven't written for several days, but
I have not forgotten you! It has been more peaceful,
so I have been going out to ride my bike. I never get tired
of being outside!
      The bicycle has become the most popular means of
transportation. People pile loads of wood on their bikes.
This scares me. It reminds me that the winter will be
cold without electricity or gas.

September 1, 1993

I am going to rehearsal at noon. Afterward, Dad will take
me to audition for the vocal program at the music school.

All my activities are making life seem a bit more normal.
We should not let ourselves stagnate. We need to continue
to develop and educate ourselves because we are still a
part of Europe.

September 2, 1993

I won third prize in the radio music quiz! Tomorrow at
nine o'clock, all the winners will be interviewed live on the
radio, and then we'll all have lunch together. There is also
going to be an awards presentation. My parents will come
with me.

LOOKING BACK

The radio interview was wonderful! I felt so comfortable
and excited in the studio that I talked for a long time. After
we were off the air, the crew asked if I would like a job
with them! We just laughed.

September 14, 1993

School is back! Walking to school today reminded me of the
good old peaceful days. Yet this day is somehow surreal.

September 24, 1993

The telephones are out again, and I can't call the radio quiz. There are mornings when I get up only because of the quiz.

Mom bought me a pair of winter boots! I am lucky that she found a pair because there aren't many shoes in the stores. She bought them right away because who knows how much more they will cost come winter.

September 26, 1993

This day is special only because we've moved the hands of our watches back an hour. We are no longer on Daylight Saving Time. Actually, there is something else special about this day: Dad and I went downtown on our bicycles to see a performance sponsored by the First Children's Embassy, called *Happy Beginning of the New School Year!* There was lots of laughter, theater and songs. Occasions such as this are a wonderful escape for us.

October 1, 1993

Dad took me to the doctor, who said that the spasms in my legs won't stop until some of the shrapnel is taken out.

When I look at my scars, I think that they would be less noticeable if I could go to the beach this summer and get a tan. I look at the photos of our past summer vacations and, somehow, this helps the pain in my legs.

October 2, 1993

The electricity came on at seven o'clock this morning. Everybody was in a hurry. Bathing, washing, ironing, cooking, vacuuming and cleaning before the electricity went out again. A few hours of electricity bring us a bit of normalcy, like being able to use the elevator and to hear the sound of our doorbell. If only I could spend ten minutes of this precious time watching a video!

October 4, 1993

In today's newspaper I read an article about a five-year-old girl named Irma who will never walk again. Irma was wounded by the shell that killed her mother. She was immediately evacuated to Great Britain, where she was operated on several times. Despite all the operations, she will never walk again. She was just beginning to experience the joy of walking, running and dancing, and now she is deprived of it forever.

October 7, 1993

The mist of this October morning reminds me of a quiet, misty morning nearly one year ago when, instead of the chirping of sparrows, there was an explosion and I was wounded.

I try to imagine what that man felt and thought when he pulled the trigger. I must have been some kind of a threat to him, but how could a thirteen-year-old girl who loved school, music and just being a kid be a threat to anyone?

October 8, 1993

The electricity came on. I dried my hair with a blow dryer!

October 13, 1993

My mom and I went to my voice lesson in the electric company truck. The driver often picks up hitchhikers and bravely drives by the river. This is extremely dangerous because he has to pass through the major intersections, where snipers shoot at everything that moves. But it's the fastest way to get into the city. At the sound of bullets, we all duck—as if that's going to help.

October 15, 1993

At the Youth Theater, Palcici gave a concert for the representatives of UNICEF and for all children who could attend. Each of us received a wonderful care package. We couldn't wait to open them at home, so we opened them on the bus.

October 18, 1993

It is a year today since I was wounded. Scars and shrapnel remain, but the deepest scar is in my soul.

This morning I refused to go outside. I was afraid that my nightmare would happen again. My parents didn't seem to understand my almost superstitious fear, but they did not force me to go out. I know that no walls can protect me if it is meant to happen again. Still, one moment I was ready to open the door, and the next I wanted to hide.

After a few long hours of thinking, I convinced myself to go to school. It was a good decision because being at school greatly calmed my fears. Unfortunately, shelling started. I hid in the school for almost an hour before I dared to head home. I wasn't sure whether I was running away from the shells or toward them, but finally I got home.

Later I did my homework and played guitar. Just another day.

October 20, 1993

I went to music school, but my voice lesson was canceled because of the bombing. In the afternoon, I performed a song at an event organized by a humanitarian organization, Flowers of Love, that links children of France with us through letter writing. My grandfather, whom I had not seen for months, came to watch my performance. I could see on his face that he was very proud. I was so happy to see him.

All the children received a care package sent by a child in France. Mine came from a boy named Gregory. It was really wonderful to get some candy and school supplies, but the best gift was gaining a new friend. Gregory is now my pen pal. He writes that his little brother and mother feel for us and hope our suffering will end soon.

On our way home, Mom and I tried to hitchhike but without success. Terrible explosions echoed throughout the city. Finally a water truck picked us up and drove us halfway.

October 25, 1993

Today the daily newspaper, *Oslobodjenje*, published my essay "Dad, Don't Let Me Lose My Legs," in which I describe the day I was wounded.

If this craziness is ever over, newspaper articles, books and videotapes will tell only a small part of this genocide.

I had a chemistry test at school. I am not sure what I'm going to get. Dad went to parent–teacher night. Uh-oh! I hope he's going to be satisfied with what he hears.

LOOKING BACK

My family was lucky if we had meat once a week. A can of ground beef or tuna was a celebration.

In the early fall of 1993, Dad began making a tasty dish, apparently of wild mushrooms that he picked in the fields. He would fry them in a little oil and mustard, and we loved it.

One day while I was alone at home, I discovered a brown snail gliding up the kitchen wall. The following evening, while everyone was enjoying Dad's delicious mushrooms, I told them about my discovery. Sanel gasped and dropped his fork. Dad looked at Mom, then at Sanel and me, and confessed. "Actually, our mushrooms are snails."

For a moment we were all silent. Then, quietly, Sanel picked up his fork and continued eating. I pictured my dad, kneeling on the wet ground and picking snails, risking his life in the open fields amid zooming bullets. I smiled and quickly said, "They're delicious, Dad. Thanks."

A normal, happy childhood:

(*above*) Nadja with her mom, Jasmina, in the snow

(*top*) Nadja as a baby on holiday on the Adriatic coast

(*middle*) Baby Nadja in the Adriatic Ocean

(*right*) Young Nadja eating bread

Nadja and her dad, Sandi, in Dubrovnik

(*top left*) Nadja with her mom and brother, Sanel, on the swings in the park

(*top middle*) Nadja with Sanel on the old city wall of Dubrovnik

(*top right*) Nadja, age nine, at the family cottage in winter

(*right*) Nadja with her dad at the cottage

(*bottom right*) Nadja and her mom in Paris while on tour with Palcici, the children's choir

Nadja's class picture from fifth grade, just before the war. She and her two best friends are sitting on the first step, second (Nadja), third and fourth from the left

(left) Nadja's first concert

Nadja in front of
the National TV
and Radio station,
age fourteen

(below) Palcici back
to strength near
the end of the war

Nadja writing
in her diary

Nadja with Mom and Dad

Godina I Broj I Sarajevo, maj/svibanj 1993.

DJEČIJE NOVINE

"SARAJEVSKA

RAJA"

(far left) *Kids of Sarajevo*, the newspaper created by the children of Nadja's apartment building

(left) Nadja with the flowers she received after a book reading

Nadja in the ruins of the National Library, summer 1996

The exterior of the National Library

The presidential building after it was burned out

October 30, 1993

I've been looking at a photo album. My eyes are drawn to
the food-covered tables in the pictures of birthday parties.
I haven't seen that much food in a long, long time!
Sometimes I can't even remember the names of the cakes
and cookies that used to be my favorites.

To feel better, I read the newspapers. In spite of
everything, the Sarajevo Film Festival is on. They are
showing cartoons and documentaries, but I can't go
because of the bombing. These days I don't dare go outside.
Shells are exploding all around, but my fear makes me feel
like a coward, and that's what I really hate.

November 5, 1993

I have not been writing for a while because each day is the
same. But today is my grandfather's birthday. I can't go
visit him because of the shelling. My grandparents' phone
doesn't work, but we called their neighbors to give my
dearest grandpa the most beautiful wishes in the world.

I remember how we used to go to his house to celebrate
his birthdays. Everyone was there: children, grandchildren,
neighbors and friends. Today the lovely past seems so far
away, shoved aside by death and suffering. Our family is
scattered all over the world.

I wish you a very happy birthday, dear Grandfather.
May you have many more.

November 9, 1993

I went to school, as usual. During music class, an explosion
interrupted our song. We waited inside for a long time
because we were afraid to go out on the street. We found
out later that a shell had hit a classroom at a nearby
school. Eight people were killed, including teacher Fatima
Gunic and three of her students. Several students were
seriously wounded, and all because they bravely went to
school despite the bombings. Children were killed because
they refused to miss out on their education.

Another tragedy today: the famous Old Bridge has
been destroyed. The city of Mostar is left without
its symbol.

November 10, 1993

Today I went to the opening of the soup kitchen at my
school. I was planning to play my guitar and sing, but an
unbearable sadness made me mute. We had lunch, but
every bite was hard to swallow because, at the same time,
a memorial ceremony was being held at the neighboring
school for yesterday's victims.

Peace Please

December 1, 1993

My city is being shelled constantly. Five to ten civilians are killed every day. I can't even peek outside, and I am worried about my brother — he is working today.

December 8, 1993

I live this humiliating, no-longer-human life,
from siren to siren,
from basement to basement.
I smell fire in the air.
I see blood and victims.
Like a prisoner I watch the smoke that rises
from the buildings of my city.

December 11, 1993

Today is my cousin Jasenko's tenth birthday.
We called him on the phone and wished him
all the best in this world. We can't visit
him because of the sirens and the shelling.
We had to be satisfied with a kiss over
the phone.

December 13, 1993

My mom works every day, but now she also volunteers at
the State Hospital as a member of the Bosnian Women's
Association. She hauls water, feeds patients and washes
wounds. When she comes home, she is exhausted and sad.
I heard her saying to Dad that it tears her apart to see
the youth of Bosnia with no arms and legs. I am worried
about her.

December 24, 1993

A formal Christmas concert was held today in the Sarajevo
Cathedral. Palcici sang. The concert ended with the mes-
sage "Peace to People of Good Will!" I wish all people who
celebrate Christmas can celebrate their next holiday in
peace and happiness.

Afterward we received packages filled with candy. As
we arrived in our neighborhood, it was strangely quiet.
There was nobody on the street. A man ran by and told us
that several shells had landed nearby only ten minutes ago.

December 27, 1993

How can anyone survive? In the last five days, over twenty
thousand shells have landed on the suburb of Zuc Hill.

Do they know that they are killing not only Bosnians but Croats, Serbs and all the others who consider this country their homeland? Do they know that we help each other, that we love each other? Do they know that young people are getting married, paying no attention to religious differences, only to their hearts and character? I can't write about this anymore! It hurts too much.

December 31, 1993

This last day of 1993 goes by with intensified shelling. Four shells hit the very center of the city. As usual, the victims are civilians. Five were killed and thirty were wounded. Poor people! They only wanted a slice of bread or a piece of tomato to bring hope into the last hours of the old year and the start of the new. Instead the last moans of this bloody year are the deafening sounds of explosions.

Another war-infected year has passed. My wish is that peace reigns throughout the whole planet, that there are no wars anywhere and that I will live my life freely again. I wish that people will love each other and be loved. Finally, I wish the words I write will become more cheerful.

HAPPY NEW YEAR!

January 3, 1994

PREŽIVLJAVANJE!! —(survival)

Today, in the ruins of a house
in the Boljakov Potok suburb, five
people lie murdered by a single shell.
Downtown, an entire family of six was killed at their dinner
table. A shell made a direct hit on the wall of their dining
room. I wish I could just stop thinking about all this chaos
around me, but I can't.

January 6, 1994

The Red Cross gave us new clothes today. I received a
warm jacket, red and green tights and a pair of boots.
   I was walking home, happy, when the shelling started. I
was afraid, so I ran into the nearest building and hid in the
stairway. I waited twenty minutes for the shelling to stop
but finally decided to run home. I found my mom in tears.
She was worried about me and also mourning two friends.
They were killed today on their way home from work.

January 11, 1994

Morning. A quiet morning. The sun is shining and birds are
chirping. Suddenly, an explosion, and the glass is shattering

around me as I drop to the floor. Another explosion! I am paralyzed by fear until my mother's scream jolts me. I run to the hallway ... a third, fourth and fifth explosion — the ground beneath us is shaking madly, as if it's going to break open and swallow us. I am crying and hugging my mother. A sixth detonation, and windows in the stairwell shatter.

Then silence. The only thing I hear is my mom consoling me as I panic about my dad, who is on duty with the Red Cross. The next moment, the neighbors are running down the stairs, heading to the basement. Mothers are screaming for their children. Chaos and confusion. I see panic spread over my mother's face, but when she sees me looking at her, she tries to smile.

When I finally gather enough courage to look through the window toward my school, there isn't a soul on the street. On the steps near my school, I see a body. Later I found out it was a woman whose head had been blown off by a shell.

When Mom and I went into my room, we found a piece of shrapnel lodged in the window ledge. A big piece of glass was lying on my desk and glass shards covered my chair. Danger — death itself — had been so close!

January 22, 1994

It was a quiet January day. Snow brought children out to play
— all smiles and happiness. Then, a shell. The children could not
get home because a second shell fell right in front of them.

There was no hope for my unknown little friends Indira,
Jasmina, Nermin, Mirza, Admir and Daniel.

Many children were wounded. Eight-year-old Muhamed is
recovering at the Clinic for Children's Surgery from severe
jaw and leg injuries. The doctors are fighting to save the
legs of brothers Elvir and Admir.

I saw the picture of four-year-old Jasmina in the
obituary column. Her eyes glimmer with the eternal
question, Why?

There is no answer.

January 26, 1994

Sometimes I think that there is no hope and that we are
all dying slowly while the whole world watches silently.

They send us crumbs of food, yet never condemn those
who kill us. I am sure they could bring us peace instead of
crumbs. If they continue like this, in a few years they will

have nobody to feed. The aggressors kill children and rape women. The world looks on and perhaps gives us a thought while sitting in their comfortable homes and palaces. Are they unable to see?

On behalf of the tens of thousands of wounded children begging for help, in the name of those who have given their lives for the peace and freedom of Bosnia and Herzegovina:

WORLD, PLEASE WAKE UP AND HELP US!!!

February 2, 1994

I have not been outside since January 6. I desperately miss walking outdoors, but I can't even peek out. I do not dare because of the shooting. Every night while the shells roar, I open my window just a crack and take a few breaths of fresh air. I am starving for air.

My mom took a few days off work, so for a while I don't have to worry if she's going to get back home or not.

February 5, 1994

This is a terrible day! A shell exploded at the Markale marketplace. Sixty-eight citizens of Sarajevo killed and over a hundred wounded. A catastrophe! This evening is passing with grief and tears.

peace please help us

February 6, 1994

It's Sunday, the day of mourning. The city is ghostly quiet. There are only a few passersby on the streets of my beloved Sarajevo. Silence ...

February 8, 1994

Today is the tenth anniversary of the fourteenth Winter Games—the Sarajevo Olympics! I watched the TV footage of this spectacular event with pride and sadness. Such tragedy is happening to a place that fascinated the whole world in 1984, and to a people who united all countries and offered love and friendship to every visitor.

Why?

February 16, 1994

This day passes in peace. I can hear children shouting while sledding outside. Is this a sign of peace?

February 18, 1994

Through the window, I watch the crowd of people and children on my street, thinking how easy it would be to get used to peaceful days. Perhaps this sudden peace is because NATO has sent an ultimatum that the aggressor must cease fire and remove their tanks.

This evening I went out sledding for the first time since the war began.

February 19, 1994

The roar of NATO jets over the city wakes me up every morning. For a moment I am annoyed because they start up so early, but then I bite back my complaints — NATO might help end this war. I get up and start a new day.

Today we got humanitarian aid: beans, cooking oil and long-awaited sugar.

Great anxiety is in the air, but also hope, as we await the result of the UN ultimatum.

February 20, 1994

I am counting the hours until the ultimatum deadline. The tension increases by the minute. NATO jets are circling the city.

February 21, 1994

Last night all of Sarajevo was restless. I slept in my sweatshirt and pants. I put some cards, crackers and my teddy bear in my backpack and kept it next to my bed in case I had to run to the basement in the middle of the night. The jets were roaring over the city. The UN warned that if the ceasefire order was not obeyed and the weapons were not removed, NATO jets would strike. On the early morning news, it was reported that the aggressor partially complied with the ultimatum. So far, NATO is not going to use its force against them.

They tell us that after twenty-three months of fear and misery, we can go out on the streets, that there is no danger. With my whole heart I hope they're right.

It's hard to believe that the thought of intervening finally came to somebody after the deaths of more than ten thousand citizens of Sarajevo, including fifteen hundred children.

I am looking at these latest developments with suspicion. I don't understand much about politics, but I believe many people will be ashamed that they did not end this war sooner and save thousands of lives.

February 24, 1994

Are we getting used to peace? I have to believe it because my cousins Jasenko and Ada are coming for a visit — after two years I am going to see them again! It's as if they're coming from another world when, in fact, we've been separated by only ten miles.

(Are we any closer to peace?)

March 6, 1994

It is hard to describe my feelings these days. During the times when I could only dream about peace, my heart trembled as I dreamed of joy, happiness, flowers and music. Now that we have peace, there is nothing, no feelings at all. Have we suffered too much? Maybe we are so used to holding back our feelings that we've forgotten how to show them … or we just don't dare. I hope we will gradually make room for feelings of peace and happiness.

March 8, 1994

HAPPY WOMEN'S DAY TO ALL THE WOMEN OF THE WORLD!

Today I wish that the mothers of Bosnia and Herzegovina and the whole world get hugs and kisses from their children. I hope this will be the last holiday that so many mothers of my homeland celebrate away from their dearest children!

Is it a coincidence that today, after almost two years, the tram made its first circuit around my beloved Sarajevo? Even if it is a coincidence, this is a special gift for mothers. The atmosphere is hard to describe. Your heart trembles the first time you hear the tram. The people are so happy — they wave to the driver. Some shed a tear. An indescribable fragrance of peace is in the air.

March 13, 1994

A happy Eid to all people of the Islamic faith! I wish that all people of my country will be able to celebrate their holidays in unity, peace and happiness.

March 16, 1994

Can you imagine the beautiful feeling in my heart while I'm sitting and writing in my own room? Since we have no heat in our apartment and our little stove warms up only the kitchen, my room has been a storage room. Cold and damp have made green mold stains on my walls. After wiping them off, I taped up some posters of my favorite band, U2. I put toys, books, photo albums and a globe on the shelves. Now

I finally have my own place. The old green clock is here
with me. He seems to strike louder when it's time for
school. When I go to bed, he strikes more softly, as if
he's singing a lullaby.

And now, the joke of the day:

We are getting some variety in our diet. One day we eat
red beans. The next day we eat black beans. Then the next
day we eat red beans. The next day we eat black beans ...

March 18, 1994

TODAY IS A BIG DAY FOR BOSNIA AND HERZEGOVINA!
Today in Washington, DC, the Bosnian-Croat Federation
agreement was signed. Many politicians from around
the world were present, including the president of the
United States, Mr. Bill Clinton.

March 19, 1994

A few days ago, I saw a group of UN soldiers on TV. From
the backpack of one soldier, a stuffed panda peeked out. At
that moment I felt a tingle in my heart. Can you imagine! A
hardened soldier with a toy in his backpack? How does it
feel to come to a country at war and maybe never return
home? Each of these soldiers has left a sorrowful mother,

father, wife or girlfriend. The soldier with the bear probably
left his child behind. At the last moment, perhaps a little girl
gave her father her favorite toy to keep him safe. So the
panda goes everywhere the soldier goes. Whenever he has an
idle moment, the soldier holds the bear and thinks about
his family.

I hope that all the UN soldiers can soon go back home
to their families because there will be no need for them
to protect us.

March 20, 1994

Winter is counting its last hours. In the afternoon there
was a soccer game between the UN Protection Force and
Club Sarajevo. It was held at the city's largest stadium.
My dad invited me to come along, but I am afraid of being
in such a large crowd.

The atmosphere was so beautiful and festive! I could
feel it even just watching the game on TV—the fans
cheering, flags flying, the band playing.

But, after the game, they showed some images
of past Sarajevo massacres on the news.
Sadness never leaves us.

March 21, 1994

The most beautiful and cheerful season begins
today. Rosy and delicate spring—birds, sun and buds
showing on the few trees that are left. The people are
radiant and cheerful. Today every living being falls in love
with life, nature and everything beautiful that surrounds us.

March 24, 1994

Peace slowly seeps into the pores of my life and heart. On
my way to school, I looked at the bombsite where I was
wounded. It is such a dark and ominous place. There was a
whole muddle of feelings inside me. I felt joy because it
was peaceful again, but at the same time a powerful
tremble went through my body as I remembered the shell
that exploded so close to me. I made an effort to allow
only the good feelings, and I walked on to school. In my
mind hung a sentence: May I not forget, and may it never
happen again.

March 30, 1994

The bombings have stopped, but the snipers are still at
work. I still walk extremely fast and run across the
intersections. On the way to my voice lesson, I crunched

countless pieces of glass under my feet.

Today I saw the building known as the "Match Box."
When it was bombed, all the apartments burned. The
TV footage was haunting — people trapped by the fire
climbing out of the building through windows. Today the
only thing that remains is a tall skeleton with gaping holes.

April 5, 1994

Today I have two pieces of sad news and one piece of
happy news. The first: today is the second anniversary
of the death of Suada, the first victim of the war. Also,
the already tortured city of Gorazde has suffered heavy
bombing.

After these sad thoughts, the good news hardly brings
any comfort, but perhaps it will offer a bit of hope.
Tonight, after nearly two years, some of the streets of
Sarajevo will be lit by streetlights.

April 21, 1994

The citizens and defenders of Gorazde are struggling
through their worst day. Hundreds of people have been
killed. Twenty were children.

Nothing is being done to help. The world just sits
and watches.

April 24, 1994

The situation in Gorazde is finally getting better. People are organizing the transport of the wounded to Sarajevo, where they hope to receive medical care.

I feel like a worthless crumb in a mountain of things. My life is meaningless. When there is electricity, I watch a movie and see that children in other parts of the world are entitled to a future as soon as they're born, while both adults and children of Bosnia have to fight for their future with their own blood. I can't understand why this is happening.

May 2, 1994

I try to picture what it will be like one day, after the war, when the refugees return to their homes. Many will find only ashes. I imagine that the reunions of those who stayed and those who fled will be extremely emotional and sad. A little girl will have become a young woman and not recognize her father. A man will run toward his wife, desperately needing to hold her and his two-year-old son, but the little boy will not understand. He will barely even look at the strange man.

After all that has happened, there will be even more sadness.

LOOKING BACK

Due to my frequent appearances on the radio, sharing my poetry with my fellow citizens, I was offered to host a small morning radio show called *The Music Box*. I spoke about famous composers and various musical instruments. I also played my guitar, sang and read entries from my diary. I quickly realized that sharing parts of my diary created a sense of solidarity and understanding between me and the suffering citizens of my beloved Sarajevo. This sharing ultimately resulted in something truly incredible.

May 4, 1994

Guess what? No, not an A in math—something far more sensational. You're now in print! I know this sounds unbelievable, but there you are lying on my desk—*Sarajevo Childhood Wounded By War*. I am extremely excited. I think it's wonderful to have my own book. You should see the cover. I really like it. There will be a reading on May 17.

May 17, 1994

The reading was just as wonderful as I imagined it. The underground hall of the K55 Theater was crammed full of people I love and respect. During the event, my heart was stirred by many different emotions, including a feeling of deep loss and sadness. The theater director, Gradimir Gojer, said, "All this is a part of an enormous debt to those who are no longer with us." I looked around at the faces of hundreds of my fellow citizens, and I realized that we're all one family deeply wounded by war. Still, we're all fighting bravely.

At the end, my eight-year-old friend Biba presented me with a bouquet of white and purple violets. How is it possible that in a city where there is no food, no water, no electricity and so much death, there are flowers? We have flowers for the burials of our loved ones and for my book reading!

May 23, 1994

Thanks to the Red Cross, we now receive a glass of milk and a sandwich for lunch at school. This kind gesture makes me think of the good old days. In peacetime, an older person would sigh and say, "Those were the good old days!" I never really understood their nostalgia. Now when I think back to when I would take a walk with my friends and buy a delicious sandwich or ice cream for lunch, I sigh and say, "Those were the good old days!"

May 29, 1994

It's Sunday. Sporting events are taking place in the city, including a bike race. It is uplifting to see the colorful sea of people gushing through the streets. Still, I am very fearful, and I don't dare join this large gathering. I don't trust that the aggressors would spare us from bombings. I will trust them only when it's safe for us to go skiing in the mountains that now hold their tanks and weapons.

June 19, 1994

Today, in the seemingly peaceful Sarajevo, there is more death and sadness. Four people in a tram were wounded by snipers. A passerby was also killed next to the Holiday Inn hotel. Dad and I had walked by the hotel just minutes before the man was killed. Just when peace lures people outside, some monstrous atrocity happens, and I hear a warning voice: Nadja, the war is still here!

July 13, 1994

It is my mom's birthday today. She received some perfume, but my gift for her made everyone laugh. I found several boxes of different sizes and placed them inside each

other. The smallest box was a purple box for a ring. Inside
I placed a note that read:

"Dearest Mom, for your birthday, I wish you a lot of
imagination! HA, HA! And, of course, I wish you joy and
harmony in the house. Happy Birthday!"

August 5, 1994

Dad painted the walls of my room. Still, their stark
whiteness seems false to me. Freshly painted walls cannot
make me forget that just days ago they were covered in green
mold from the damp and black soot from the wood stove.

August 6, 1994

Today I saw a play called *Sarajevo Scenes*, showing stories
of our survival. There is a lot of humor that seems deeply
sad because we see our own bleak reality in it. Still,
laughter is a welcome balm to soothe our pain.

August 24, 1994

I will soon have to audition for the Music High School, and
I am nervous about it. I really want to study music, but I'm
not sure if I will do well at my audition.

August 28, 1994

Great news! I am accepted to the Music High
School — I was the best auditioner, with 112.5 points.
I am so excited, but still I shouldn't brag because I have a
long path of hard work and dedication before me.

September 3, 1994

My choir friends and I visited the Pediatric Hospital
today and sang for all the little patients. It was nice, but
I was overwhelmed by sorrow just looking at all the
sickly children.

Just before our performance, we established a satellite
connection with a humanitarian concert in Helsinki, and
part of our performance was broadcast to thousands of
concertgoers.

October 8, 1994

Today the snipers shot at another tram. Although he was
fatally wounded, the driver steered the tram several
hundred meters out of danger before he succumbed to his
wounds. Fifteen civilians were also wounded.

Life is sad and terribly cruel, isn't it?

October 18, 1994

Two years have flown by since the day I was wounded. The
scars and shrapnel in my legs do not allow me to forget.
Still, if I knew that tomorrow the war would end, my
wounds would hurt less.

October 31, 1994

A strange tension hangs over the city. I heard sirens
several times, and the radio warns about a possible bomb
attack. Everyone in the house is restless and worried.

November 8, 1994

Several children were killed and wounded yesterday. A
thirteen-year-old girl was sitting in her room when a sniper
shot her in the neck. They rushed her to the hospital. I
saw it on TV. It was a chaotic scene filled with the noise
and bustle of people trying to help her. At one point, the
woman who was holding the girl's head screamed, "She's
alive! She's alive!" The girl opened her mouth, desperately
trying to breathe. She blinked once, twice and then
forever faded.

November 19, 1994

I am terribly sad that my inspiration and need for writing
comes from massacres and tragedy. At first glance,
yesterday was a regular day. But November 18 was the
last day for seven-year-old Nermin, the last time he
looked at the sun and the sky. He was walking with his mom
when a sniper shot both of them. His mom is seriously
wounded, but I am sure that the gravest hurt of all is
in her motherly heart. A single bullet cut off Nermin's
existence. With tears and sorrow, I will always remember
Nermin and his last walk.

November 24, 1994

At night, black and gloomy thoughts invade me instead of
sleep. In the darkness, images of bloody, dead children
revolve in front of my eyes. One image after another
forces itself upon me. I feel such pain and humiliation
that I cry and cry.

I don't even have the right to dream anymore. For God's
sake, I am only fifteen!

December 1, 1994

Every day there is blood and sirens. The aggressor has cut
our supply of gas. We get no electricity and water only by
the spoonful. I am depressed by all this, and I cry a lot. I
am disgusted by this war. The thousandth
day of our oppression is coming soon.

January 4, 1995

It's dawn. Snowflakes are dancing in the wind. A few
moments later, they melt on my window. I look up and
watch the snowflakes dancing again. They dance and then
melt. I'm watching a battle of life and death. All goes
in circles.

January 24, 1995

Two Dutch journalists came to visit me today. Their goal is
to make several documentaries about the children in this
war and their creative ways of surviving.

   One of the questions they asked me was, Which parts of
my life would interest children my age in Holland? I think
these children would want to know how we have survived
while everything around us is being destroyed.

February 2, 1995

It is peaceful in Sarajevo. The trams are in service. There is water, electricity and sometimes even gas. I am deeply thankful for this, but I dream of running on the beach. I would give anything to hear the sound of the sea.

March 12, 1995

There was heavy bombing downtown last night. A doctor was killed when a bomb landed right in her apartment. Another person was wounded.

On the TV station broadcast by the aggressor, two dead children were shown. The report said that the children were shot by a sniper from our defending army. I am terribly disturbed and shaken by this event and by the loss of these children. Children on all sides are innocent. Adults must bear the responsibility for these tragedies.

March 14, 1995

The trams are again out of service. The war rages on with no end in sight. What hurts is that this life seems normal. I am so used to living in these conditions that I can't even imagine that people in other countries actually walk calmly across an intersection instead of making a mad dash.

March 25, 1995

Today I performed in a concert organized for children whose fathers lost their lives defending Bosnia. The hall was filled with mothers and their fatherless children. As I stood on the stage looking out into the audience, I saw so many tear-filled eyes. These children never deserved to suffer so terribly! Some are just babies — maybe they've never even seen their fathers.

After the performance, every child received a monetary gift, but no amount of money can lessen their sorrow.

April 3, 1995

I have some news! We are moving to another apartment! Climbing to the fourteenth floor several times a day has become extremely exhausting for all of us. Mom is very tired from walking to work and back and then having to climb fourteen flights of stairs. We are going to trade apartments with a lady who wants to be closer to her relatives in our neighborhood. Her apartment is downtown and on the first floor! This will be great — my music school is a five-minute walk away.

April 25, 1995

So many things are weighing me down. In truth, I don't even know if writing will make me feel any better.

My brother is stranded in another part of the city because of the heavy bombings. He finally got through on the phone to let us know he is all right.

The bombings of the city have intensified, so school has been canceled until May 8. This tough time feels even tougher without friends. Many of my friends live only three tram stops away, but they might as well be on the other side of the world. I feel ashamed that I cry so often, but the tears keep welling up.

Then I think of all those people who immigrated to other countries. Some complain about how much they suffer, but at least they have safe shelter, food and water. Even if they were on the streets with one piece of bread, they would be lucky because they don't have to fear that a bomb will kill them.

Freedom. It seems like any other word, but how much longing and need it holds!

This madness has to end someday, but when, God, when?

MIRIS SLOBODE !!!!??
(fragrance of freedom)

April 30, 1995

A four-month ceasefire ends tomorrow at noon, but it was just a fake promise on a piece of paper. Hundreds of adults and children were killed, crippled and wounded during it. What kind of ceasefire was that?

May 5, 1995

We've moved to our new apartment, and we're almost finished unpacking. I think my room is the prettiest, but I have no desire to run to the window and see my new neighborhood. There are fewer and fewer people in the streets. Around nine o'clock every night, silence swallows the city and every citizen anxiously awaits … something.

I wish I could take my bike and ride around, but fear overwhelms me. Besides, my mom would die of worry. Sanel is out somewhere — he didn't tell Mom where he is going, so she just waits and worries. God, how many mothers have waited for their sons until the early hours of the morning, only to receive a dreadful phone call from a hospital or morgue?

Words are useless to describe my sadness, humiliation and misery.

May 23, 1995

I just heard a bomb zoom above our building. The
telephones are out, and I can't talk to my family and
friends. I've gotten into the obsessive habit of lifting the
phone receiver to listen for a dial tone. I do it over and
over — I want to be the one to announce the great news
that the phones are back on.

There is nothing but silence.

May 26, 1995

Something truly gruesome and terrible happened yesterday.
There was a massacre in the city of Tuzla: sixty-three
people dead and hundreds wounded. All the victims were
between the ages of three and twenty-five — so many
young people brutally killed while the "peacekeepers" and
the UN do nothing. I am disgusted. They refuse to bomb
the tanks that killed the innocent citizens of Tuzla, yet
they are supposed to be protecting the city!

May 27, 1995

Mom stormed into my room around eleven o'clock last
night. She woke me up, handed me my slippers and made

me run with her into the hall. Dad and Sanel were already there. Three bombs had exploded only a few blocks away. The fourth exploded so close that they could hear the shrapnel and shattered glass showering our building. It's amazing that I slept through it all!

Soon, the neighbors from the upper floors came down as well. We all sat in the hallway the rest of the night. Ambulances and fire trucks rushed by. Life is so fragile.

Dad just brought the *Oslobodjenje* newspaper. The death toll in Tuzla is now 66 with more than 236 wounded. Twenty dead bodies are yet to be identified because they've been mutilated beyond recognition. The radio announcer has been reading the names of the young people who were killed.

All of us are frozen in sadness at the images of dead youth. I weep for all the victims. No matter what their religion or ethnic background, all of them stayed in our homeland, sharing sorrow just as we once shared happiness. Today's young Bosnians don't allow their different faiths to come between them. We know that we can and must live together. The aggressor obviously cannot grasp this.

June 6, 1995

Bombs are exploding all over the city. My family is so anxious
that even an innocent comment can trigger an argument. I
hide my feelings from everyone, but I am drowning in
despair. When will this war end? For how long will my life
consist of the dead space between two explosions?

I think all the chores and activities that we do during
the war are done to create an illusion of comfort and
normalcy. I move from room to room, corner to corner,
desperately seeking a safe place.

God, when will it all end?

June 13, 1995

My life consists of two things: the days of the past
scratched out by sorrow and pain, and the days yet to
come but sure to be the same. I don't know how many
more days will be scratched out on my life's calendar.

I wish my family could live on a tropical island covered with
banana and coconut trees. I would hardly ever stop swimming.

June 16, 1995

Explosions echoed throughout the night and into this
morning. We didn't go to the basement. If we went every

time there was a bombing, we would be living like rats.

At night I sleep for an hour or so, until an explosion shakes me awake. My heart beats madly, and it takes more than an hour to fall asleep again. Then there's another explosion, and it starts all over again.

June 19, 1995

I no longer sleep in my bed. I am afraid, so I sleep on a mattress by the front door. Yet a girl in France or America sleeps peacefully in her bed and dreams of tomorrow.

Why can't we all live together in peace instead of fighting wars? No country is worth a child's tear, let alone a child's life.

I wonder if I will ever see my two best friends again. Sanja escaped to Germany and Nevena to Australia. If I do see them, what will our first meeting be like? I try to imagine it, but it seems absurd. What could I tell them? How do I explain that while they lived in safety, hundreds of children lay in puddles of their blood, screaming? I fear there would just be silence and emptiness between us.

July 6, 1995

I cannot describe the despair that smothers Sarajevo.
Yesterday a neighbor was killed on my street. A bomb
exploded right in front of him. His wife ran into the
street, crying, screaming and tearing her hair out. The
other neighbors quickly picked up his body.

Only minutes later, several children carrying empty
water canisters stepped right over the puddle of blood
and kept going. The struggle called life continues and
time cruelly marches on.

July 8, 1995

Today I received the news of the death of my dear friend
and former neighbor, Tarik Dzankovic. He was a wonderful
human being who always greeted me with a smile. He had
beautiful dark eyes with long eyelashes.

Tarik was brave, determined and stood firmly for jus-
tice while defending those who were hungry and thirsty.
He was always helping elderly neighbors carry water or
bags up the many flights of stairs in our old apartment
building.

One afternoon, I was on my way to choir rehearsal and
I saw him coming home from the front carrying a huge

backpack. He was obviously tired, but he smiled and asked how I was. That boyish smile hardly ever left his face. On the day of his death, he was proudly defending human liberty.

My feeling of loss is too big for words. What remains are his crying parents and brother and all of us who loved him.

July 10, 1995

I try to play the piano, but my weary fingers slip off the keys. I take up a book and try to concentrate, but my thoughts mix up and I don't know what I just read. There is so much horror and chaos, and I need to think, think and think before I understand any of it. But I don't want to think! I don't want to cry! I want to laugh, but there's nothing in Sarajevo to laugh about. I am so tired of all of this.

July 13, 1995

If there were peace, I would be wearing a beautiful summer dress today. I would be smiling and offering my mom a bouquet of roses, a card and a lot of kisses. Today is my mom's birthday. My mother, who walks to work stalked by bombs and bullets, who miraculously

makes delicious meals out of nothing, and whose hair is
going gray from worry. It was heartbreaking to see my
mom crying on her birthday.

July 14, 1995

There has been a loathsome crime — genocide against the
civilians of Srebrenica. Tens of thousands of civilians
experienced their worst nightmare as the aggressor took
over the city. The UN watched and did nothing; the rest
of the world closed its eyes. The world doesn't want to see
its own shame, yet it doesn't want to help the victims
either. On TV they showed a little girl who was raped and
an eighty-year-old woman who was beaten and forced to
march for hours in the burning sun.

July 30, 1995

Yesterday was my birthday. I was in a good mood. Some
friends visited and brought small gifts and big hugs. It
was one of the rare "normal" days, and I was filled with
optimism and cheerfulness.

But on the day I wore my prettiest skirt, smiled and
received kisses and gifts, others were mourning. In

yesterday's newspaper I read a memorial of a boy named Nedzib Gojak, whose birthday would have been the same as mine had he survived this war.

August 5, 1995

I don't know if this is very typical among people living through a war, but before I fall asleep, dreadful images of bloody bodies appear before my eyes. In the morning I remember nothing in detail, but the horror remains. Sometimes at night, like a child, I call my mom to come and talk to me. Her voice comforts me and dispels the darkness and heavy thoughts.

August 6, 1995

Sometimes I wonder if this is really me — the cheerful girl who went to sixth grade and loved shopping and going to the theater. That girl of twelve is infinitely different than this crushed sixteen year old in her worn-out clothes who aimlessly stares out the window. I ask myself, Why am I sitting at my desk when the sun is shining outside? Where are my suitcases packed for summer vacation? My questions mock me. I give too much freedom to my thoughts! I want to force them down, tie them, enslave and control them. But I can't. I can't even control my eyes that aimlessly stare at nothing. The only things left are my emotions, and I must keep hold of them. If I let them loose, they will flood everything around me: this notebook, this desk and even the sun, which mercilessly burns my cheeks through the window.

I wonder if I will always exist in some middle space between the painful memories of my past and the reality of my present — searching for the future.

Nadja

New Hope

Ever since I was wounded, my parents had been trying to get me out of the city. Finally, in mid-August 1995, we received a letter from one of the humanitarian organizations in Croatia that my parents had written to for help. I had been chosen as one of twenty young Bosnians to go to America. Thanks to the partnership of two organizations, Women of Bosnia and Project Shelter, I was to fly from Croatia to the United States and live with an American family. We didn't know much else, but we were overjoyed! Just a week later, we received another letter informing us that I would have to be in Zagreb, Croatia, in five days; otherwise, I would miss my flight to the United States.

Suddenly we felt hopeless. The only way to leave the city was through an underground tunnel, which had been dug during the second year of the war. The tunnel was the only way to bring in food and medicine, and the government granted exit permits mainly to soldiers, nurses and dangerously wounded civilians. It rarely allowed children to leave. The presence of children in the city motivated the adults. Without their children to fight for, they might have given up hope.

For three days my mother went to the presidential building and pleaded with an official to grant us permits to leave. It was no use. On August 27, 1995, we decided to leave Sarajevo illegally.

My uncle, who was a soldier, gave my mother his sister's identification document — she was a nurse and allowed to go back and forth through the tunnel without being questioned. To get more sympathy, my mom put a pillow around her waist so she would look pregnant. I wore pigtails, trying to look twelve or thirteen.

My father drove us to the ramp where the tunnel started. This open space was one of the most dangerous parts of the city, almost completely surrounded by the aggressor. A long line of people were waiting to be checked by the police. They were exhausted and indescribably miserable, with no shelter from the attacks.

After an hour, my mom and I were finally at the front of the line. We had no permits, but we were hoping that the soldier in charge would have pity on a pregnant nurse with a child. He looked at my mother's papers and nodded his approval. Then he looked at me.

My mother could go, the soldier said, but I could not. My papers showed that I was sixteen, which meant that I had to have my own permit. My mother begged him to let me go, but the soldier's word was final. No matter how sad the story or how desperate the need, one tiny piece of paper showing your name, age and designated time to leave was all that counted. We returned home defeated.

That night, as soon as I closed my eyes, I could see the faces of the pale and emaciated people waiting in the line. There was no hope in their lifeless, watery eyes, and this frightened me the most.

The next day I was alone in the apartment. Uneasy thoughts and haunting images were still racing through my head. Suddenly there was a deafening explosion. I heard the shattering of windows and, a moment later, people on the street below frantically screaming for help. I threw myself on the floor, holding my hand over my mouth so I wouldn't scream. Ambulance sirens and the cries of the dying filled the air. And somewhere out there were my parents ...

A few minutes later, my father came home with a loaf of fresh bread. I hugged him tightly — I could have lost my father for a few slices of bread.

My mom came home from work a bit late, but in her eyes I saw a flicker of hope. Just as the bomb hit, she was at the presidential building for the fourth time asking for our permits. Everyone in the building became frantic as they got news of the massacre. The worker, who was already frustrated with my mother, grabbed two forms and filled them out — our permits to leave that night between seven and ten o'clock. We would never get a second chance.

The shells were roaring incessantly. It was insane to drive through the city — I wasn't even sure that I wanted to go. One moment I felt ready to risk my life on the streets, but the next I saw my father forcing himself not to cry. Still, Mom and I packed my things. I looked around my room, whispering a good-bye to my dolls, books and piano.

We silently carried the suitcases to the car. I nervously looked around — we were the only people on the street. The whole time in the car, I sat curled up in the back seat naively thinking I was safer that way.

At the ramp we saw the same long line of desperate souls, now being soaked by rain. Bombs were exploding some fifty yards away, but the people in the line barely budged. Suddenly a shell exploded very close to us. My whole body shook, and I screamed at the soldier sitting in the guard hut. "How can you just sit there while shells are falling all around us? How can you be so merciless and cold? Hurry up, for God's sake. Hurry up!"

In a sharp voice the soldier replied that he wasn't protected either and that we were all doomed to die. People in the line looked at me sadly but said nothing. My father embraced me and walked me to the nearest building. He told me to wait there. Then he walked back and stood in my place, ready to sacrifice his life for mine.

Finally we were checked by the soldier and taken to a crowded basement to wait for the tunnel to open. Even though my father was not going with us, he was allowed to come to the basement. We waited for more than an hour because the tunnel was so narrow that people could only walk in one direction at a time. I overheard someone saying that snipers shot at people coming out the other end.

When my mom recognized a neighbor in the crowd and told him that we didn't have a ride at the other end, he pointed to a man standing in the corner, the driver of the truck our neighbor was taking. My father went over to the driver, and, though I couldn't hear what they were saying, I could see the man hesitating. A few minutes later, he shook my father's hand and smiled faintly.

The moment of saying good-bye came suddenly. We had only a moment. As I stepped into the tunnel, I turned to look at my father one last time. Only darkness stared back.

The next moment I was walking in a narrow passage reeking of urine and sweat. The tunnel was about five feet high, so I had to hunch down or I would hit my head. Dirt and water dripped on us, and we slogged through ankle-deep mud. I was carrying two bags and a backpack, and they seemed to get heavier with each step.

You couldn't stop to rest because there was someone one step in front and someone one step behind. When people passed out from exhaustion or lack of air, others would try to carry them, but the stream of people trudging through the miserable tunnel never stopped.

We walked for thirty minutes, but it seemed like the longest walk of my life. The wounds on my legs were hurting and my back was aching. I just wanted to give up. I turned around and looked at my mother. Her frail frame was carrying even more bags than I was. She looked at my tearful eyes and smiled. She said, "Remember, Nadja. Remember your dream and keep walking!" I turned around and sped up.

At the end of the tunnel was a shallow trench. Even when we ducked, the walls were not high enough to protect our heads. With every flash of lightning we were visible and in great danger from the nearby snipers. We had to be absolutely quiet, but my heart was pounding so loudly that I was sure they could hear it.

We finally arrived in the suburb of Butmir. Walking through the city was extremely dangerous, as bombs were continuously exploding and snipers could see us every time the lightning flashed.

In the trench, a young soldier had offered to help us with our bags. Now he was walking beside me. Every time there was an explosion nearby, he would grab my hand and say, "Don't worry. Just keep walking, keep walking!" My mom was behind us. Whenever I heard a bullet, I'd turn back to see if she was alive. She would whisper, "Keep walking, Nadja! Keep walking!"

We finally got to the truck — six men, my mother and me. Every bit of our clothing and luggage was soaking wet. Around eleven at night, we were in a convoy waiting to go up Mount Igman. The road was so narrow that cars could move only in one direction at a time. Before the war, Igman was famous as the site of the Winter Olympics. Now it was surrounded by snipers, so we could travel only at night.

While we waited, my mother went on a mission. The night before, when we tried to leave illegally, my uncle, the soldier, took my guitar so we'd have one thing less to carry. When we were denied access through the tunnel, he brought the guitar to his house in Butmir. The convoy was waiting about two miles from his house, so my mother decided to get my guitar. I was horrified — was she really going to walk two miles, with shells and bullets flying, for a guitar? No mere thing was that important — only our lives were. Mom wouldn't listen to me. She just said, "Nadja, you can't leave without your guitar!"

An hour passed. The rain poured down, and I could hear the constant roar of thunder and shells. I could barely breathe, terrified that my mother was lying somewhere injured or dead. Finally she reappeared, carrying my guitar. I just held her as she shivered.

Around midnight we started our forty-five-minute trip up Mount Igman. The driver maneuvered very slowly and carefully without headlights so the snipers could not see us and would have to shoot randomly. No one said a word. We just listened for the sound of rocks slipping beneath our tires. One wrong move and we could plunge over the edge of the cliff.

Finally the driver turned on the headlights — we were past the greatest danger. Relieved, everyone (except me) lit up a cigarette. I started talking compulsively, making up for those forty-five minutes of silence.

No one was killed or injured on the Igman road that night. Perhaps the heavy rain discouraged the snipers. But we later heard that the night before, when my mother and I had tried to leave, seven people were killed there.

Outside Sarajevo, safe from snipers and bombing, Mom and I got off the truck because the men were traveling in another direction. After we said our good-byes, I looked around and saw a small grocery store. Even though the doors were locked up tight for the night, there was a bunch of bananas hanging in front. I blinked once, twice and then looked again. Yes, they were just hanging there, as if they were not one of the world's greatest luxuries!

The next day, Mom and I hitchhiked to Croatia. We spent a day recovering from our journey, and then I flew to the United States. The last I saw of the war and of my old life was my brave mother waving good-bye, hiding her tears behind a smile. She made the return trip down the deadly mountain and again through the misery of the tunnel to rejoin my dad and brother. Three months later, Sanel took the same route to the United States. My dear parents still live in Sarajevo.

Nadja's tunnel permit

The escape tunnel
is now a museum,
which Nadja visited
in 2004

(right) Nadja
revisiting the
tunnel

(far right) The exit
from the tunnel
in Butmir

Nadja's original diary

Afterword

By the time the war ended in December 1995, an estimated 250 000 people had been killed. Many thousands of these lives could have been saved had enough people around the world insisted that their leaders intervene. I am thankful that the war finally ended, but sorrow and pain still roam the streets of Sarajevo.

The war happened not only to the Bosnian people but to all of us. The peoples of the world — all nationalities, ethnicities and religions — are limbs of a single body, and when one of us is hurt, we are all in pain.

Since the war in my country, countless acts of war, terrorism and violence have plagued our world, and it is easy to feel hopeless and overwhelmed. When I become discouraged about my work for peace, I think back to the tunnel. There, just when I was about to give up, my mom made me realize that I had the strength to get through the darkness. "Remember your dream and keep walking!" she had said. Not a day passes when I don't hear her words in my heart.

All of us have our own tunnels to walk through. All of us have our own dreams and visions to fulfill. But our common dream is that of a world of peace and tolerance, in which we're respected and embraced for who we are. For this dream, we walk through the mud and darkness together because, in the end, the tunnel will take us to the world we want to live in.

We must remember our dream and keep walking!

Acknowledgments

My deepest love and thanks go to my husband, Chris Morrison. Thank you for believing in me from the moment we met and for walking with me ever since. I would like to thank my extraordinary family — my parents, Jasmina and Sandi, and my brother, Sanel, who taught me hard work and perseverance by their example. Lots of love and gratitude go to Richard Burck, my wonderful friend and mentor, for reminding me to always keep walking. Thanks to the Morrison family, and especially to Jules for all her love, help and hugs. I would like to thank my two wonderful host families, the Yeagers and the Simons, for welcoming and loving me like their own child. I can never thank them enough.

Many thanks to Kevin Wolfe, who believed in my diary long before it was translated into English. Loving thanks go to John Robbins and his family for their constant inspiration, goodness and love, and to Grant Vecera, who has inspired me to write without knowing it.

Thank you to Marie Bartholomew and Charis Wahl, my designer and editor, who worked to realize my dream for this diary. Charis, thank you for making the journey of publishing my first book less daunting. Thank you to Valerie Hussey, for challenging and believing in me;

to Sheila Barry, for our many comforting conversations; to Ned Morgan, for his insightful contributions; and to all the staff at Kids Can who contributed to this project.

Finally, my love and thanks go to all my friends and family, whose love and care have always nourished me. I have been blessed in all of you.

May we live in peace and sow tolerance for the future generations!